Sugar Gliders

by Elizabeth O'Sullivan

Lerner Publications Company • Minneapolis

In memory of my father, Terry

The images in this book are used with the permission of: © ANT Photo Library/Photo Researchers, Inc., pp. 4, 8, 24, 26, 27, 28, 29, 30, 31, 32, 48 (top); © Laura Westlund/ Independent Picture Service, p. 5; © Joe McDonald/Visuals Unlimited, pp. 6, 7, 16; © A. Harmer/Peter Arnold, Inc., p. 9; © Daniel Heuclin/NHPA/Photoshot, p. 10; © Dave Watts/Alamy, pp. 11, 18, 46; © Gerry Ellis/Minden Pictures/Getty Images, p. 12; © Krystyna Szulecka/Alamy, p. 13; © age fotostock/SuperStock, p. 14; © Joseph Van Os/Riser/Getty Images, p. 15; © A.N.T. Photo Library/NHPA/Photoshot, pp. 17, 22; © Dwight R. Kuhn, p. 19; © Belinda Wright/Oxford Scientific Films/Photolibrary, p. 20; © Ken Lucas/Visuals Unlimited, p. 21; © Kathy Atkinson/Oxford Scientific Films/Animals Animals, p. 23; © Alan & Sandy Carey/Photo Researchers, Inc., pp. 25, 35; © Roland Seitre/Peter Arnold, Inc., p. 33; © Ern Mainka/Alamy, p. 34; © Patti Murray/Animals Animals, p. 36; © Tony Bock/Toronto Star/ ZUMA Press, p. 37; AP Photo/The Free Press, Mankato, John Cross, p. 38; AP Photo/Wally Santana, p. 39; © Uma Sanghvi/Palm Beach Post/ZUMA Press, p. 40; © Carolyn A. McKeone, p. 41; © Jason Edwards/National Geographic/Getty Images, p. 42; © Biosphoto/Klein J.-L. & Hubert M.-L./Peter Arnold, Inc., pp. 43, 48 (bottom); © Bill Coster WF/Alamy, p. 47.

Front Cover: © A.N.T. Photo Library/NHPA/Photoshot.

Lerner Publications Company
A division of Lerner Publishing Group, Inc.
241 First Avenue North
Minneapolis, MN 55401 U.S.A.

Website address: www.lernerbooks.com

Library of Congress Cataloging-in-Publication Data

O'Sullivan, Elizabeth, 1973–
　　Sugar gliders / by Elizabeth O'Sullivan.
　　　　p.　cm. — (Early bird nature books)
　　Includes bibliographical references and index.
　　ISBN 978–0–8225–7891–8 (lib. bdg. : alk. paper)
　　1. Sugar glider—Juvenile literature. I. Title.
QL737.M373O88 2009
599.2′3—dc22   2007029228

Manufactured in the United States of America
1 2 3 4 5 6 – BP – 14 13 12 11 10 09

Contents

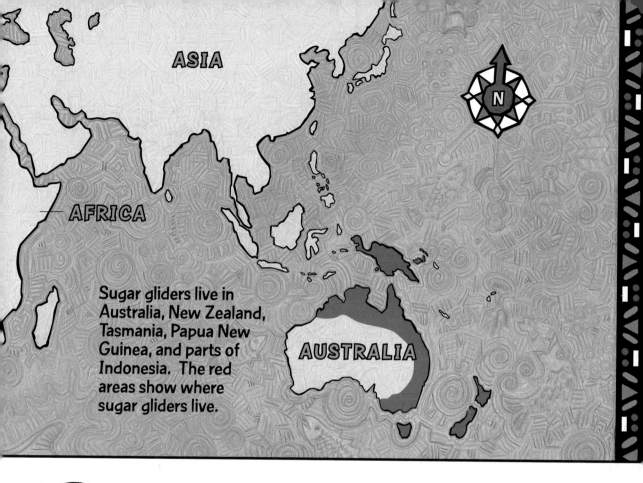

Sugar gliders live in Australia, New Zealand, Tasmania, Papua New Guinea, and parts of Indonesia. The red areas show where sugar gliders live.

Be a Word Detective

Can you find these words as you read about the sugar glider's life? Be a detective and try to figure out what they mean. You can turn to the glossary on page 46 for help.

arboreal	larvas	opposable
colony	mammal	predators
dominant	marsupials	scent gland
exotic pets	nectar	tame
joeys	nocturnal	territorial

Chapter 1

This sugar glider is getting ready to jump from a branch. What will happen when it jumps?

Gliders, Not Flyers

 A small animal sails through the air. It looks like a flying squirrel. But it is not a squirrel at all. It is a sugar glider.

A sugar glider cannot really fly. But it can glide a long way. A sugar glider can sail more than 150 feet through the air. That is half as long as a football field.

A sugar glider sails through the air.

To glide, a sugar glider climbs to a high place in a tree. Then it jumps. It stretches out all four legs. This opens up flaps of skin that run from its ankles to its wrists. These flaps catch the air like a kite. The glider uses its flaps and its bushy tail to steer. It lands on a lower branch.

Scientists call sugar gliders Petaurus Breviceps. *Petaurus means "rope dancer." The animal got this name because of the way it moves through the trees.*

Sugar gliders have very long tails. Their tails help them steer as they glide through the air.

A sugar glider is about 1 foot long. That is the same size as a gerbil. The glider's tail takes up at least half of that length. An adult sugar glider weighs only about 4 ounces. Most hamburgers weigh that much!

Several of the glider's back toes are joined together. This makes a "hair comb." The glider scratches its fur with it to keep clean.

Sugar gliders have sharp claws. The claws let them hang onto smooth bark on trees. Sugar gliders also have opposable (uh-POH-zuh-buhl) thumbs and big toes. These move and grab like a person's thumbs. This helps sugar gliders grab branches.

Sugar gliders' eyes are large. They can see well in the dark. That's important because gliders are nocturnal (nahk-TUR-nuhl). That means they are awake at night. They sleep during the day.

Sugar gliders have large eyes so they can find food at night.

A sugar glider has soft fur. A young sugar glider has gray fur on its back and sides. Tree sap stains the fur brown as the animal grows. A glider's face has three stripes. The dark middle stripe runs all the way down the sugar glider's back.

The folds of skin on the sugar glider's side help it glide. The skin spreads like a kite when the glider stretches its legs. When the legs are curled up, so are the folds of skin.

When a sugar glider climbs on a tree, it can look a lot like a squirrel. But it is more closely related to a kangaroo.

Sugar gliders may look like squirrels, but they are actually more like kangaroos. Kangaroos and sugar gliders are marsupials (mahr-SOO-pee-uhls). Koalas and opossums are also marsupials.

This kangaroo is a marsupial. Its baby is sticking out of its pouch.

Marsupials carry their babies in a pouch on their bodies. Marsupials are a kind of mammal. All mammals have hair and feed milk to their babies. People are mammals too.

Sugar gliders live in the wild in Australia, New Zealand, Tasmania, Papua New Guinea, and parts of Indonesia. Some people keep sugar gliders as pets.

Wild sugar gliders often live four to five years. Pet sugar gliders can live as many as 14 years.

Sugar gliders live in rain forests, like this one in New Zealand.

Chapter 2

Sugar gliders play on a tree. What else do they do in trees?

Forest Home

Would you like to climb a tree and never come down? Sugar gliders do that. They are arboreal (ahr-BOR-ee-uhl). Gliders sleep, eat, and play in the trees. They sail through the air from tree to tree. They hardly need to touch the ground.

Staying in the trees helps to keep gliders safe from predators (PREH-duh-turz). Predators are animals that eat other animals. Owls, cats, dogs, and other animals eat sugar gliders.

Sugar gliders also stay safe by living together in family groups. A family group is called a colony (KAH-luh-nee). Each colony lives on about 1 acre of land.

Groups of sugar gliders play and live together.
Each group has its own piece of land.

Sugar gliders share the trees with other gliders in their colony. But they will not share with other colonies. Sugar gliders are territorial. That means others are not welcome in their trees. Males will attack sugar gliders from other colonies that come into their area.

Sugar gliders can be loud when they are upset. They can screech and hiss.

These sugar gliders are sleeping in their nest. Many sugar gliders will share one nest.

Gliders sleep together in a nest. They make the nest in the hole of a tree. They use leaves to make their nest soft. Gliders hang upside down from branches to pick the leaves. They hold onto the branches with their back feet. They pick the leaves with their hands. Then they wind their tails around the leaves to hold onto them.

Sugar gliders cannot glide through the air while carrying leaves in their tails. They need their tails free to steer while gliding. Instead, they run along the branches. Their tails carry the leaves as they run. Then the sugar gliders line the nest with the leaves.

Sugar gliders use leaves to make their nests soft.

Chapter 3

This sugar glider is eating sap from a tree. How does the sap come out?

Sweet Meals

Sugar gliders are named for their favorite food. They eat lots of sweet, sugary tree sap. Sap is a dark, sticky liquid. It is always flowing inside a tree. But it oozes out if the tree has a cut.

Sugar gliders sometimes bite tree trunks to make a cut. Sap comes out, and the sugar gliders eat it. They eat the sap of eucalyptus (yoo-kuh-LIHP-tuhs) trees, acacia (uh-KAY-shuh) trees, and gum trees.

Sugar gliders eat the sap of eucalyptus trees, like this one.

Sugar gliders also eat the flowers and juice from eucalyptus trees.

Sugar gliders also find sweet food in flowers. Sometimes they eat the whole flower. Sometimes they just eat the flower's juice. This juice is called nectar. The sugar glider's favorite nectar comes from flowers that grow on eucalyptus trees.

23

*Sometimes sugar gliders eat bugs. This sugar glider
is eating a praying mantis.*

Not all the food sugar gliders eat is sweet.
Sugar gliders also eat bugs. They can catch
spiders or insects such as flying moths. And
they eat larvas. Larvas are baby insects. They
look like small worms.

Sugar gliders' ears help them find food. Their ears are very sensitive. They can hear the softest sounds. Sugar gliders even hear the tiny sounds that bugs make. Then they can find and eat the bugs.

Sugar gliders can hear very well. They use their hearing to find bugs to eat.

It can be hard to find food in the winter. In winter, gliders spend more time cuddling together every day. They often cuddle instead of playing or looking for food. Cuddling uses less energy than moving around. So they do not need as much food as when they are busy.

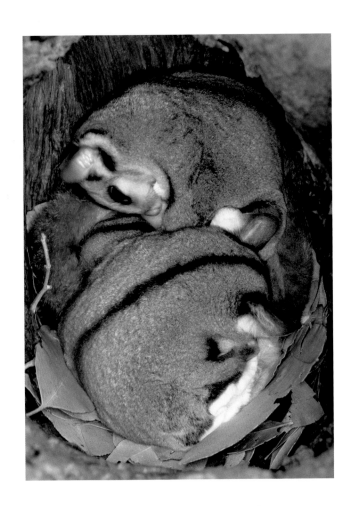

This sugar glider family is sleeping. Sugar gliders sleep more in the winter.

Chapter 4

A baby sugar glider rides on its mother's back. What are baby sugar gliders called?

Tree Families

Marsupial babies are called joeys. A female sugar glider gives birth to one or two joeys at a time. She does this once or twice every year.

A newborn sugar glider is tiny. It weighs only about 0.007 ounces. A dime weighs as much as five of these babies!

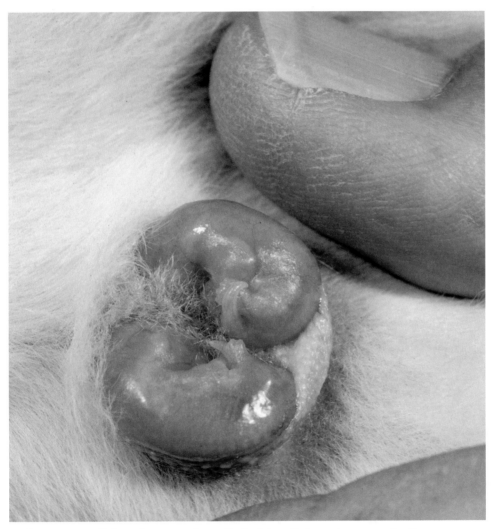

Baby sugar gliders have only a little bit of time to grow before they are born. These sugar glider twins are very young.

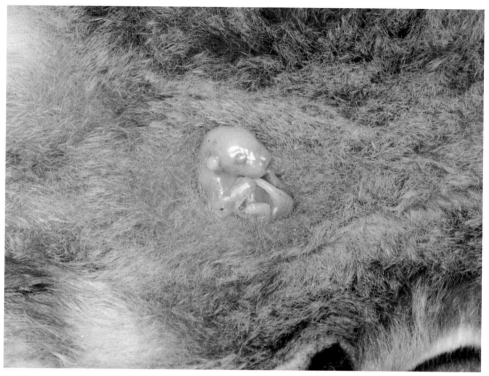

This joey is asleep in its mother's pouch.

A newborn joey cannot see. Its eyes are still shut. But it has to make an important trip. Once the joey is born, it must crawl through its mother's fur. It crawls to the pouch on her belly. The baby makes this trip only once. Then it stays in her pouch and grows. The pouch has milk for the baby. And the pouch keeps the baby safe.

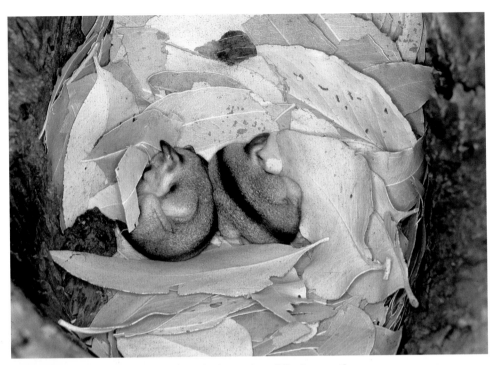

These joeys are sleeping in their nest. Their mother and father both care for them.

A joey lives in its pouch for 70 days. That is more than two months. Then it can leave the pouch. Soon its eyes open. But it doesn't go far. The joey stays in the colony's nest in the trees.

Mother sugar gliders care for their joeys. The fathers help too. Fathers snuggle with their joeys in the nest. And they help keep joeys clean.

When joeys are almost four months old, they start to explore. But they do not leave the nest by themselves. They ride on their mothers' backs. Joeys hold their mothers' fur tightly. Together they move through the treetops. Then they return to the nest.

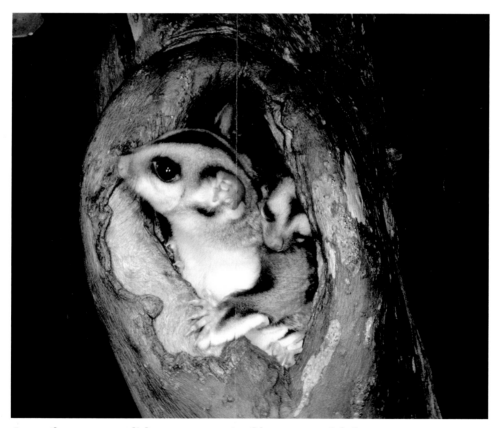

A mother sugar glider comes out of her nest with her joey on her back.

Joeys drink their mothers' milk until they are about four months old. Then they are weaned. This means they stop drinking milk and eat the same food as adults. They are learning to take care of themselves.

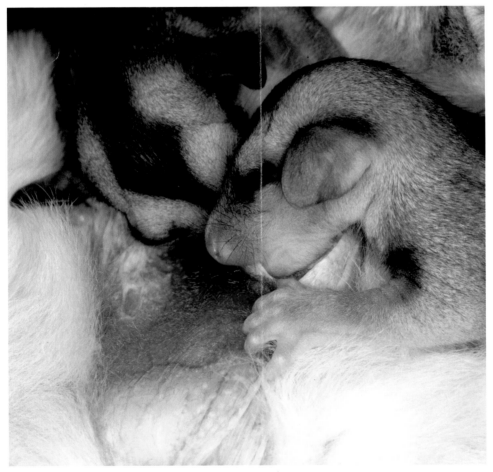

These joeys are drinking their mother's milk.

When they are old enough, sugar gliders leave the colony. They start their own colony.

Most sugar gliders leave their colony when they are about 10 months old. Then they form a new colony. And they can have babies of their own.

Sugar glider colonies have one male that becomes the leader.

Not all sugar gliders become parents. One or two males in each colony become fathers. The others do not. A male that becomes a father is the dominant (DAH-mih-nuhnt) male. The dominant male acts as a leader.

Males have a scent (SENT) gland that makes a special smell. The dominant male rubs his scent gland on all the gliders in his colony. That puts his smell on each of them. This smell tells other sugar gliders who is in their colony.

Sugar gliders smell each other to see if they are both from the same colony.

Sugar gliders talk to one another. They make many sounds. At night, they often bark like dogs. When they are upset, they make a loud sound. It sounds like a chain saw! They chirp when they are content.

Sugar gliders have loud voices. When they are scared, they can alert the rest of the colony.

Chapter 5

This sugar glider is used to people. Can sugar gliders be kept as pets?

Sugar Gliders and People

A sugar glider can be a fun pet. It has soft fur. It snuggles during the day. And it plays in the evening. Some gliders ride on their owners' shoulders. They can jump off shoulders. Then they glide through the air.

These sugar gliders are tame. They have always been pets. But not all sugar gliders are tame.

But other pet sugar gliders never become tame. They do not get along with people. Some bite.

Sugar gliders are called exotic (eg-ZAH-tihk) pets. This means most people think of them as wild animals. But some people want to keep them as pets.

Other animals have lived with people much longer than sugar gliders have. Dogs and cats have lived as pets for thousands of years. People know all about dogs and cats. But they do not know as much about sugar gliders.

Sugar gliders have not been kept as pets for very long. Recently, they have become popular in Taiwan (above), *an island in Asia.*

Owning sugar gliders is against the law in some states. In other places, it is against the law to let pet gliders have babies. In the United States, people must get special permission first. Then they can let their sugar gliders have babies. And they can sell the babies.

This sugar glider is at a fair in Florida. Its owner is trying to sell the gliders he has bred.

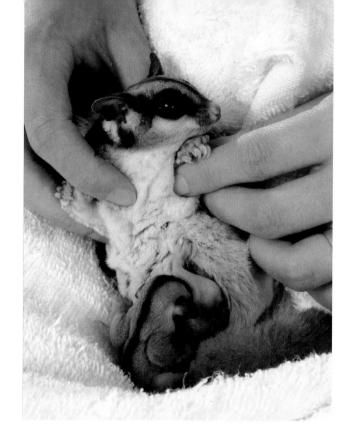

Sugar gliders need a lot of care. A sugar glider is not the right pet for everyone.

Sometimes people do not know how to care for pet sugar gliders. Some pet gliders die because their owners do not take care of them.

People in Australia are worried about that. In Australia, it is against the law to sell gliders as pets. But it is allowed in New Zealand. People catch sugar gliders there. They keep some as pets. And they ship some to North America to be sold as pets there.

Adult sugar gliders that were born wild are brown. Those that were born in cages are gray. Tree sap has not stained their fur. Gray sugar gliders sometimes make better pets. They have spent their whole lives around people. So they are used to people.

This sugar glider is gray because it was born in a cage. Its fur was not stained by tree sap.

Many sugar gliders are losing their homes. People are cutting down the forests where they live.

People have caused trouble for wild sugar gliders. They have cut down some forests where sugar gliders live. This leaves those gliders without homes. There are not as many wild sugar gliders as there used to be.

Even so, many sugar gliders still live in forests. They snuggle. They find sweets to eat. They sail through the air. They are wild and free.

A NOTE TO ADULTS
ON SHARING A BOOK

When you share a book with a child, you show that reading is important. To get the most out of the experience, read in a comfortable, quiet place. Turn off the television and limit other distractions, such as telephone calls.

Be prepared to start slowly. Take turns reading parts of this book. Stop occasionally and discuss what you're reading. Talk about the photographs. If the child begins to lose interest, stop reading. When you pick up the book again, revisit the parts you have already read.

BE A VOCABULARY DETECTIVE

The word list on page 5 contains words that are important in understanding the topic of this book. Be word detectives and search for the words as you read the book together. Talk about what the words mean and how they are used in the sentence. Do any of these words have more than one meaning? You will find the words defined in a glossary on page 46.

WHAT ABOUT QUESTIONS?

Use questions to make sure the child understands the information in this book. Here are some suggestions:

> What did this paragraph tell us? What does this picture show? What are some special things about a marsupial? Where do sugar gliders live? What do sugar gliders eat? Can sugar gliders really fly? What is your favorite part of the book? Why?

If the child has questions, don't hesitate to respond with questions of your own, such as What do *you* think? Why? What is it that you don't know? If the child can't remember certain facts, turn to the index.

INTRODUCING THE INDEX

The index helps readers find information without searching through the whole book. Turn to the index on page 48. Choose an entry such as *food*, and ask the child to use the index to find out what sugar gliders eat. Repeat this exercise with as many entries as you like. Ask the child to point out the differences between an index and a glossary. (The index helps readers find information, while the glossary tells readers what words mean.)

LEARN MORE ABOUT
SUGAR GLIDERS

BOOKS
Arnold, Caroline. *Australian Animals*. New York: HarperCollins, 2000. Find out about other Australian animals in this book. The animals are grouped by where they live, such as in the forest or desert.

Kalman, Bobbie, and Heather Levigne. *What Is a Marsupial?* New York: Crabtree Publishing Company, 2000. Read about different marsupials from all over the world.

Sill, Cathryn P. *About Marsupials: A Guide for Children*. Atlanta: Peachtree Publishers, 2006. Learn more about marsupials. This book is easy to understand and has illustrations of marsupials in the wild.

Weber, Belinda. *The Best Book of Nighttime Animals*. Boston: Kingfisher, 2006. This fully illustrated book explains why some animals are active at night.

Wightman, Caroline. *Sugar Gliders: A Complete Pet Owner's Manual, 2nd rev. ed.* Hauppauge, NY: Barron's Educational Series, 2008. This guide includes drawings, photographs, and information about how to take care of pet gliders.

WEBSITES
Australian Animals
http://www.ausinternet.com/ettamogah/australiananimals.htm
Visit this site to learn more about Australian wildlife. There are photos of animals, games to play, and other activities.

Marsupial Mammals
http://www.ucmp.berkeley.edu/mammal/marsupial/marsupial.html
This site has information and photos about the marsupial family.

Sugar Glider
http://www.enchantedlearning.com/subjects/mammals/marsupial/Sugarglider.shtml
See a labeled drawing of a sugar glider, and read more about what it eats, what animals eat it, how it moves, and more.

GLOSSARY

arboreal (ahr-BOR-ee-uhl): living in trees

colony (KAH-luh-nee): a group of animals that lives together

dominant (DAH-mih-nuhnt): being in charge of the group

exotic (eg-ZAH-tihk) pets: normally wild animals that are kept as pets

joeys: babies of animals that have pouches

larvas: baby insects that look like worms

mammal: an animal that has hair and that feeds its babies milk

marsupials (mahr-SOO-pee-uhls): animals that have pouches, which hold their babies

nectar: sweet juice from inside a flower

nocturnal (nahk-TUR-nuhl): active at night

opposable (uh-POH-zuh-buhl): able to be placed against other fingers or toes. A sugar glider's thumbs are opposable. So are a person's thumbs.

predators (PREH-duh-turz): animals that hunt and eat other animals

scent (SENT) gland: a body part in the skin that makes a certain smell

tame: able to live comfortably and safely with people

territorial: protecting a home area

INDEX

Pages listed in **bold** type refer to photographs.